Amanda says
NO to DRUGS,
NO to BULLIES
And Teaches
Other Kids to Say
NO to DRUGS TOO!

Written by Jim Rauth
Illustrated by Mark Morel

ISBN-10: 1515201325

ISBN-13: 978-1515201328

Dedication

This series is dedicated to all people who have the disease of addiction. Who know loneliness and loss of self-control that only someone with the disease can truly understand. To my best friend Michael Lubahn who taught me loyalty and left this earth too soon from the grip of this disease. And to his two children that were left behind.

I feel these difficult discussions should not wait until the fifth grade such as the D.A.R.E program, and should be discussed with your child as soon as possible. We know that if you have the disease your child's chances to have the disease infinitely increase. We also know that 1 out of 13 people develop addictions regardless of DNA. We also know when the parent or parents or care givers are involved with these conversations drug use decreases.

When doing drug and alcohol counseling I have heard clients starting use as early as age 8 and all national statistics start reporting at age 12 when it's the ship for these conversations already have sailed.

I also ask this question: Why do we reach outside of ourselves to make ourselves feel better? With the right insight, we can look inside, and surpass what the world has to offer.

Jim Rauth

Amanda, her grandmother, and her new friend, Jake, were looking at the elephants at the zoo. Amanda was sharing with them how upset she was that her mom was staying in the drug and alcohol treatment center again.

Amanda's mother Jane was back at the treatment center for her addiction to pain killers for the second time. She went to visit her mom with grandmother but Amanda likes to call her grandmother "Nana."

Amanda asks a couple of questions,
"Do you know what a treatment center is?"

(A treatment center is where people go to get
help for their addiction. People can have
addictions to drugs, alcohol, food, video games,
computers, television, exercise, gambling and
other things too.)

Do you know what an addiction is?

(An addiction a disease in the brain when
somebody keeps doing something they don't
want to do over and over again and they lost the
ability to stop doing it on their own.)

Amanda's nana said, "Amanda you know that addiction can happen to anyone it doesn't care what race you are, how rich or poor you are, or even where you live." Your mother is doing the best she can and is doing very well. She will be coming home soon.

Jake was born with one leg shorter than the other, so Jake walks with a limp.

Amanda's nana dropped Amanda and Jake off at Ella's house for a friendship party! Ella is one of Amanda's best friends in the whole world.

Jake and some other boys and girls were there. Jake wasn't dancing. Everyone was dancing and having fun. Ella yelled to Jake, "Let's dance!", but Jake just leaned against the wall.

Later that evening, all the boys and girls met at the mall. They walked through the mall looking at all the stores. Ella bought a pair of shoes. Amanda looked at a bright red dress, but it was too small.

Then Jake said, "Here Amanda take this", and Jake handed Amanda one of his mother's pain pills. Amanda said, "No, I don't want this, Jake, and you're not supposed to have this!"

Jake kept saying, "Amanda, just take one."

Amanda said, "No Jake, I'm going to be a doctor when I'm older and I'm going to help others. I don't want something that affects my thinking or judgement - and my mother is in a treatment center because she can't stop taking these. I don't want any part of this Jake."

Jake fell down and everyone thought Jake was pretending to be hurt. Jake wasn't pretending, though: he had taken one of the pain pills, and it affected his balance.

Jake hit his head on the floor and received a large lump on the back of his head. An ambulance had to take Jake to the local hospital.

Amanda asks, "Why would you want to avoid taking something that makes you feel different?"

(You could have an accident by falling down like Jake, or it could even make your heart stop beating if you take too much!)

The next morning, Amanda visited Jake in the hospital. "How are you Jake?" asked Amanda. "I'm okay," Jake replied.

Amanda said, "Jake you're one of my best friends, but we can't be friends until you get healthy and I know you're not taking pills or drinking alcohol or smoking marijuana anymore."

"I want to get better," said Jake. Jake continued, "I don't ever want to do drugs again."

The next morning Amanda gathered all her friends at her nana's farm. Amanda started teaching her friends what to say if they were offered drugs by other people.

Then the other kids had ideas too. Natalie said, "My parents have a drug test kit and they check to see if I have taken drugs every week!"

"I don't take drugs because I want to have a good future and work as a police officer. If I got caught, I couldn't be an officer." said Eric.

Amanda said, "Those are great boundaries and reasons to tell people why you won't use drugs!"

Amanda asks you, "What else you might say to someone who offers you drugs?"

(This is a great spot to work on how to say, "I can't use drugs, I want to have a healthy positive life.")

Meanwhile Jake started to get help for his drug problem at the treatment center from a doctor that worked there. Jake discovered he was using drugs to help him not feel bad.

He was feeling bad because some of the kids at school were bullying him because he was new at the school and because of his special shoe that helped him walk.

Later, Amanda went to visit Jake at the treatment center. They sat on a park bench and Jake explained to Amanda how some of boys and some of the girls were picking on him at school.

"They have been bullying me because of my one leg being shorter than the other and because I'm new at school," said Jake.

The next day Amanda gathered all the boys and girls together who were bullying Jake.

Amanda said, "How would you feel if someone bullied you?" as she held up a smartphone in one hand and tablet in the other.

"These are wonderful tools we can look for information or we can use them to communicate with our friends but we don't use them to hurt each other."

As Jake started to recover from using drugs and alcohol, he began to eat and sleep healthier. He even started to exercise and he started to play soccer.

    Amanda and her friends decide to have some fun and they went on a canoe trip. They went down the river and through the mountains.

They were having so much fun. As they went around the bend in the river they were heading toward a big waterfall. The canoe started to move faster and faster towards the tall waterfall. Everyone in the canoe started to become so frightened.

The canoe started to rush faster and faster towards the edge of the waterfall. No one knew what to do.

Then Jake stood up and said, "We have our life jackets on, we have to jump into the water and swim to the shore."

So all the boys and girls jumped into the water. And swam to shore just as fast as they could. They all made it to shore just before the canoe went over the edge of the waterfall.

Later that evening, everyone gathered around the campfire.

Amanda, Natalie and Ella all at the same time shouted, "Jake, you are our hero!"

Jake said, "No, I'm not a hero, I'm just a kid who wants to help others. I'm so grateful I received help for my addiction. Now I don't let the bullies bother me – I am who I am!
Like, when your boat is going over a cliff, it's time to jump out and start swimming!"

Just as the flames of the campfire reached real high into the air, Amanda's mom and nana appeared at the campfire.

Amanda said, "I'm so glad everyone is here. This place is so beautiful because of each and every one of you are here.. I'm glad Jake is healthy again and you are too Mommy."

"And nana and me are so proud of you Amanda for helping all the kids to understand that all children need to get along with each other and not bully each other and not use drugs," said Amanda's mom.

  Amanda came home from the camping trip with her mom. She was so glad that her mom and herself were back home living together again.

  And they started to plan their next camping trip. They decided they would take Jake along on the next trip but they would be leaving the canoe at home.

"So kids, say no to drugs and bullies, don't be afraid to feel feelings and if you need help for an addiction ask for help."

For more information:
@laughoutnow
http://BeHappyLiveNOW.com
stellarwork@gmail.com

Made in the USA
Middletown, DE
11 September 2024